FAMILIAR
Epistles BETWEEN
WILLIAM
HAMILTON
OF GILBERTFIELD
in Cambuslang
AND
ALLAN
RAMSAY
in Edinburgh

Page from the Old Parish Records of Cambuslang recording the funeral expenses of Lieutenant William Hamilton of Gilbertfield (at Lettrick) in May 1751.

FAMILIAR
Epistles
BETWEEN
WILLIAM
HAMILTON
OF GILBERTFIELD
in Cambuslang
AND
ALLAN
RAMSAY
in Edinburgh
⌘ ⌘ ⌘
with an extract from
HAMILTON
OF GILBERTFIELD'S
version of
Hary's WALLACE

Edited with an Introduction by DUNCAN GLEN
with Prefaces by R. K. D. MILNE
and NEIL R. MACCALLUM

akros

Kirkcaldy : 2000

First published 2000
AKROS PUBLICATIONS
33 Lady Nairn Avenue
Kirkcaldy, Fife, Scotland, UK
Selection and Introduction copyright © Duncan Glen 2000
Preface copyright © R. K. D. Milne 2000
Preface copyright © Neil R. MacCallum 2000
All rights reserved
Typeset by Emtext [Scotland]   Printed in Scotland
A CIP Record for this book
is available from the British Library

ISBN 0 86142 104 3

ACKNOWLEDGEMENTS

My thanks to R. K. D. Milne and Neil R. MacCallum for their encouraging Prefaces. Mr Robert Taylor of Gilbertfield not only gave much information but also welcomed me to Gilbertfield as he also did Mr Milne and Mr MacCallum. I thank Mr John King, Secretary to Strathclyde Building Preservation Trust, who accompanied Mr Milne and myself to Gilbertfield Castle, for data on the castle. I thank Mrs J. McColl, Local History Librarian for North Ayrshire Council, for help with the history of Ladyland and, as so often in the past, my thanks to the librarians of Edinburgh Central Public Library, Kirkcaldy Public Library, The Mitchell Library, Glasgow, The National Library of Scotland and The Scottish Poetry Library for helpful assistance. The extract from the Old Parish Records of Cambuslang is printed by permission of the Glasgow and History archivist in The Mitchell Library. My thanks to all who have subscribed to this edition prior to publication. As always my wife gave much guidance.

CONTENTS

Preface by R. K. D. Milne, page 5

Preface by Neil R. MacCallum: The Braes o Fame, page 7

Introduction by Duncan Glen
1 Lieutenant William Hamilton of Gilbertfield *in Cambuslang*, page 13
2 Gilbertfield Estate and Castle *and their surroundings*, page 18
3 Allan Ramsay *of Edinburgh*, page 24
4 The verse form of the epistles of Hamilton and Ramsay, *and their place within the Scottish literary tradition*, page 30

Three Familiar Epistles between William Hamilton and Allan Ramsay, page 39

Extract from William Hamilton of Gilbertfield's version of Blin Hary's *Wallace*, page 55

Bibliographical Notes, page 57
List of Subscribers, page 59

PREFACE

By R. K. D. MILNE

PROFESSOR Duncan Glen, historian, poet and publisher, has become renowned not only for his own works, but for identifying and encouraging recognition and appreciation of Scots whose contribution to Scottish culture has been mostly disregarded in recent years—in addition, of course, to modern writers. He is a Scottish nationalist, not in the narrow political understanding of the word, but in the wider sense, in that not only does he have confidence in his own native ability for creative art, but he has the humility to recognise it in others. Thus he has become the acknowledged authority on Hugh MacDiarmid, long before he became accepted in the public domain.

Another major contribution he has made to Scottish culture is to recognise the importance his native Cambuslang played in Scottish history—for this has been neglected over the past century by the industrialisation of the area. With the passing of this latter era, he has produced two major historical works—*A Nation in a Parish* and *A New History of Cambuslang*, and it is from these works that this present book emanates.

Gilbertfield Castle stands forlorn in a field at the foot of Dechmont Hill, but he has stimulated interest in it, and its most famous inhabitant, Lieutenant William Hamilton. The importance of William Hamilton to Scottish literature is not only in his own works, but for his influence on Burns and for his verse epistles with Allan Ramsay, the Scottish poet and father of one of our foremost eighteenth-century British portraitists.

Like Allan Ramsay, Duncan is maintaining national traditions by writing Scots poetry and preserving the work of Scottish poets, not only through his own independent publishing company, but by his work for the Scottish Poetry Library.

History seems to be repeating itself with Hamilton and Ramsay's connection between Cambuslang and Edinburgh; for now we have Duncan Glen and Neil MacCallum actively involved in the publicising of these Epistles—the former through their publication and the latter with his staging of "Wi Allan and wi Gilbertfield".

CAMBUSLANG
SEPTEMBER 1999

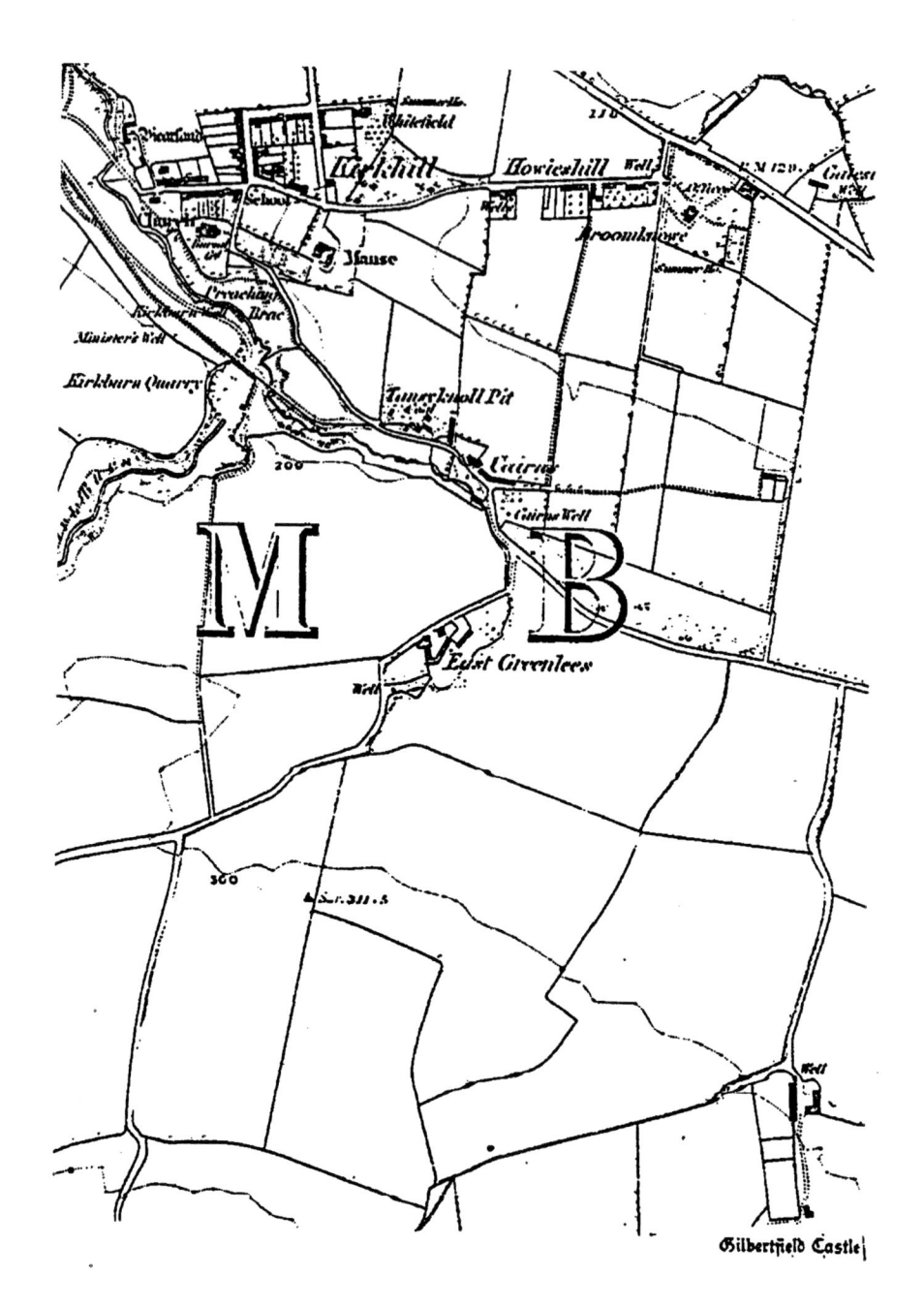

Kirkhill, Cambuslang, from Ordnance Survey Map of 1858

PREFACE

THE BRAES O FAME
by NEIL R. MACCALLUM

I HAVE NO reason to suppose that until recently my knowledge of Lieutenant William Hamilton of Gilbertfield, which was limited to the spasmodic appearances he makes in a handful of anthologies, was other than typical of the average poetry-loving Scot. His inclusion in such volumes tends to be patronising and the editors thereof dismiss him as an obscure, if interesting, footnote in the literary history of Scotland. It is instructive to cite a few random examples of this approach.

Maurice Lindsay, in his *History of Scottish Literature*, 1977, 1992, is more generous than many other commentators when he refers to "The Last Dying Words of Bonny Heck, A Famous Greyhound in the Shire of Fife" as the most significant piece in James Watson's *Choice Collection of Comic and Serious Scots Poems* which came out in three parts in

Detail from the title-page of the second edition of the first part of Watson's anthology.

1706, 1709 and 1711. Lindsay is less impressed by Hamilton's verse epistles to Allan Ramsay when viewing Gilbertfield's side of the exchanges "as little more than gentlemanly rhyming compliment". Tom Scott, who edited *The Penguin Book of Scottish Verse*, 1970, is grudging in his recognition of "Bonny Heck" as "beginning a craze for mock elegies on animals that were taken up by Burns to some effect". Scott further asserts that poetry of this genre is trivial in subject-matter and that it reflects a "deepening provinciality of language", as if the poets alone were obliged to accept prime responsibility for the considerable economic and political pressures that had brought this situation about.

David Craig, in *Scottish Literature and the Scottish People 1680-1830*, 1961, tends to focus only on Hamilton's role as an influence on another, later, greater bard, Robert Burns. This draws attention to Gilbert Burns singling out "those excellent new songs that are hawked about the country in baskets, or exposed on stalls on the streets", and Craig believes that the songs and poems of William Hamilton and Allan Ramsay, termed somewhat inaccurately "Edinburgh wits", would have been known to the poet and his brother. We can be certain that Burns thought he was in the earlier poets' debt, for in his epistle "To William Simson, Ochiltree", he hopes

> to speel,
> Wi' Allan, or wi' Gilbertfield,
> The braes o' fame;

There are, thankfully, available to us less dismissive opinions about the Laird of Gilbertfield's literary abilities, ones that judge him as a poet in his own right. Harriet Harvey Wood, who edited Watson's *Choice Collection of Comic and Serious Scots Poems* in two volumes, 1977, 1991, assesses Hamilton's verse correspondence with Ramsay as "among his more important literary achievements" and in "Bonny Heck" she sees "a further link in the chain which connects such poems as Henryson's 'Fables', Lyndsay's 'Testament and Complaynt of the Papyngo' and 'The Mare of Collingtoun' to Burns' 'The Death and Dying Words of Poor Mailie'. It has been described as 'a poem which is of no great intrinsic excellence, but derives its chief importance from being a link in the order of succession in Scots poetry' (J.H. Millar, *A Literary History of Scotland*, 1903). This is to do it less than justice. The poem has a freshness and finish which distinguish it from many other similar productions of the period (in contrast to poems such as 'The Mare of Collingtoun'); the 'doggishness' of the dog's character is well and sympathetically portrayed. Heck lives in the imagination as a dog, not as a pseudo-human being; there is nothing horse-like about the Mare of Collingtoun."

In literature as in life, we can be perfectly happy to accept sweeping assertions about certain periods in our cultural history, assuming that oft repeated, second-hand opinions represent a measured and definitive analysis. An example of this fairly typical thinking occurs in Tom Scott's introduction to *The Penguin Book of Scottish Verse*, "the seventeenth century is a poetic wasteland, few birds being heard to sing although the jackdaw clacked loudly enough in the pulpit."

Page from the edition of Watson's anthology copied by Harriet Harvey Wood for her Scottish Text Society edition of *A Choice Collection*.

The Laſt DYING WORDS of
Bonny *HECK*,
A Famous Grey-Hound in the Shire of *Fife*.

Alas, alas, quo' bonny *Heck*,
On former Days when I reflect!
I was a Dog much in Reſpect
   For doughty Deed:
But now I muſt hing by the Neck
   Without Remeed.

O fy, Sirs, for black burning Shame,
Ye'll bring a Blunder on your Name!
Pray tell me wherein I'm to blame?
   Is't in Effect,
Becauſe I'm Criple, Auld and Lame?
   Quo' bony *Heck*.

What great Feats I have done my Sell
Within Clink of *Kilrenny* Bell,
When I was Souple, Young and Fell
   But Fear or Dread:
John Neſs and *Paterſon* can tell,
   Whoſe Hearts may bleid.

They'll witneſs that I was the Vier
Of all the Dogs within the Shire,
I'd run all Day, and never tyre:
   but now my Neck
It muſt be ſtretched for my Hyre,
   quo' bonny *Heck*.

As a consequence, we were forced to accept that little work of artistic merit was available to us from seventeenth- and early-eighteenth-century Scotland. It was an era artistically ignored and best written off.

I should perhaps have questioned some of these simplistic attitudes myself before circumstances forced me to do so. My discovery of the period's literary worth came about in the following way. Tessa Ransford, then editing *Lines Review*, asked me to review *Four Poets of Cambuslang and Dechmont Hill 1626-1990* (Akros Publications, 1996) edited by Duncan Glen. In my subsequent notice[1] I stressed that "Poetry can perform many functions and of these its role as a vehicle for the recording

---
[1] *Lines Review*, no.139, December 1996, pp.59-60.

of social history should not be underestimated. Furthermore, if we want to find out what the partisans actually thought about the great issues of the day in bygone centuries the poet can sometimes come up with the answers. . . . A particular service is rendered by printing together, for probably the first time, all the known poems of Hamilton of Gilbertfield. He set the fashion for mock elegies in Scots and through his exchange of verse letters with Allan Ramsay constructed the foundations on which Burns would so brilliantly build. Colin Nicholson of Edinburgh University has written of Scottish literature 'as our way of speaking to each other, within and across time, because looking into it helps us to look into ourselves.' Duncan Glen is to be commended for enabling us to do just that."

A few characteristics about Hamilton's verse were pleasantly apparent now that it was possible to take in all of his surviving, original output at one sitting. Despite the intervening centuries the poems still worked, they read remarkably well, remaining fresh and full of the sort of energy that their author surely possessed himself. William Hamilton seemed a likeable figure who enjoyed practising his craft, not averse to boasting of his own abilities, yet determined to bring pleasure to an audience. I began to feel as if I had become an intimate of Gilbertfield and his social circle, being privileged to step back nearly three hundred years as a welcome guest at his tavern table.

My concern may have rested there had not Duncan Glen's diligent researches into the poetic traditions of Cambuslang and Dechmont Hill aroused a curiosity in me to investigate the environment that produced the poems. I am reasonably sure that few thinking Scots would deny the importance of land and place within our national psyche, that healthy respect for a shared set of experiences we call our history which enables us to connect with an emotional imperative.

The Merchants o Renoun are a group of poets, readers, musicians and singers who present dramatic performances of various aspects of our national literature; their normal base is the Netherbow Theatre in the heart of the historic Auld Toun of Edinburgh. "Honest Allan" was the title of the June 1998 show, a celebration of Allan Ramsay, the much-loved Edinburgh poet, playwright, publisher, editor, song-writer and wigmaker, a friend and verse correspondent of Hamilton of Gilbertfield. An epistle apiece from Hamilton and Ramsay was read as part of this presentation. Paul H. Scott, in reviewing it for *The Scotsman* (23rd June 1998), commented, "This was a splendid programme. It was far from an act of piety or a historical reconstruction, but as enjoyable as chatting with Ramsay and his cronies must have been."

A subsequent performance was "Wi Allan and wi Gilbertfield", a dramatic reading of "The Six Familiar Epistles between William Hamilton and Allan Ramsay" interspersed with music of the period on the clarsach and small pipes, alongside specially composed pieces for the event. There was genuine enjoyment from all of the troupe in giving voice once again to Hamilton's and Ramsay's words within earshot of Honest Allan's old stamping grounds. The audience quickly keyed in to the literary world of early-eighteenth-century Scotland; they were obviously comfortable in the company of both bards, Hugh MacDiarmid's seamless garment of past, present and future aye melling thegither.

I was conscious of all this when, late one July morning in 1998, I alighted from the train at Cambuslang Station ready to follow Duncan Glen's detailed directions towards Dechmont Hill and Gilbertfield. I had the impression of being in two different centuries at the same time. Yes, I was outwardly ambling towards the outskirts of Cambuslang, wending my way through neat suburban streets, whilst simultaneously covering the same ground that Lieutenant William Hamilton had assuredly ridden over innumerable times in an earlier age. A handful of memorable lines from his "Epistles" were my constant companions. An element of surprise also awaited me because preconceived notions condition us into believing that this part of post-industrial Lanarkshire is all grime, dereliction and desolation, whereas, having ascended Dechmont Hill, I was in a pleasant rural setting where further down its slopes I could visualise the Laird of Gilbertfield discharging his duties and tending his modest estate.

When inspecting Gilbertfield Castle, I concurred with Nigel Tranter's view of it in volume 3, South-West Scotland, of his *The Fortified House in Scotland*, 1962, 1986: "This fine and lofty example of the transition period between plain defensive tower and more commodious mansion has unfortunately fallen on evil times." I shared Tranter's sadness that it had been allowed to so deteriorate. It would be a nice thought to anticipate the appropriate agencies putting in place a scheme for Gilbertfield's restoration. It would be a fitting memorial to the poet whose "modernised" version of Blind Harry's *Wallace* poured "a Scottish prejudice" through Robert Burns's veins which would "boil along there until the floodgates of life shut in eternal rest".

My own experiences in exploring Hamilton of Gilbertfield's poetry in this way have led to an acceptance of his literary legacy, not only as a positive influence on our national bard amongst others, but as an accomplished poet and attractive character in his own right. There can be a danger when otherwise perfectly acceptable terms get used in a pejorative fashion. Hamilton was no doubt a minor poet in the annals of our great national literature, yet he is a minor poet of considerable import. He deserves his honoured place as one of the pioneers of the eighteenth-century literary revival that did so much to preserve a distinct Scottish identity in the otherwise dark days following the 1707 Treaty of Union. We should perhaps think of him as an occasional poet in the best sense of the word; either the busy public man or the leisured laird, cultured and well-read, turning out soundly-made verses on the margins of a happy and fulfilling life.

Robert Burns, in his epistle to Mrs Elizabeth Scott, "The Guidwife of Wauchope-House", hoped

> That I for poor auld Scotland's sake
> Some usefu' plan or book could make,
> Or sing a sang at least.

Lieutenant William Hamilton of Gilbertfield achieved those aims. ⌘

Sketch of Gilbertfield Castle
by J. T. T. Brown, 1884.

INTRODUCTION
by DUNCAN GLEN

Ladyland castle-tower
as seen by an artist before the tower was demolished about 1815

1
WILLIAM HAMILTON (c.1665-1751)
of Gilbertfield, Cambuslang

WILLIAM HAMILTON was the younger son of William Hamilton and Janet, daughter of John Brisbane. The family may have been related to the Hamiltons of Torrance and through them to David, a brother of James the first Lord Hamilton. What is not in doubt is that the poet's family owned the lands of Ardoch, near Kilwinning, from probably as early as 1600 and certainly before 1633. It has been accepted by writers on Scottish literature that Hamilton of Gilbertfield was born about 1665 at Ladyland, about a mile and a half from the village of Kilbirnie, in north Ayrshire, but my research has not found evidence that gives a date, or place, to his birth. Also, it is not certain that the poet's father was at Ladyland in 1665. It was probably about 1669 that the poet's father, Captain William Hamilton (son of James Hamilton of Ardoch) bought Ladyland from David Barclay[1]. The estate bought by the poet's father included what Timothy Pont described, in the early seventeenth century, as a "stronge touer" and some idea of what it looked like can be seen in a drawing based on a colour sketch made before the castle-tower was demolished about 1815—see above. When Captain Hamilton bought

---

[1] An earlier Barclay at Ladyland was Hew Barclay (?1560-1597) who wrote sonnets addressed to his fellow poet Alexander Montgomerie (?1545-?1610) who, like Barclay, was much involved in, to quote a nineteenth-century historian, "hatching Popish plots". Barclay died in 1597, drowning off Ailsa Craig which he, Montgomerie and others planned to take and establish as a base for a Catholic invasion. What happened to Montgomerie remains one of the unsolved mysteries of Scottish literary history.

the tower he had additions built onto it and a pedimented stone, which was built into the entrance to the walled garden of the mansion house (built between 1817 and 1821) is dated 1669 and has the initials W. H. and I (J) B.[2] In front of this nineteenth-century mansion was placed an interesting lectern-type sundial which was dated 1673 and has the unidentified initials M.P.C.

We know that Hamilton of Gilbertfield joined the army, possibly either Lord Hyndford's regiment or that of Col. Robert McKay, at an early age, but retired on half pay, after some foreign service, with the rank of Lieutenant. The role of country gentleman suited him very well; he enjoyed field sports, good food and drink. Literary historians have assumed that the poet owned the small estate of Gilbertfield, with its dwelling castle-tower, but not James Alexander Wilson, author of *A History of Cambuslang,* 1929, and my own researches lead me to agree with Dr Wilson.[3] It is possible that the poet rented Gilbertfield from a distant kinsman, the resident laird of Westburn, who was also descended from the Hamiltons of Torrance. The poet is referred to as Hamilton of Gilbertfield to distinguish him from William Hamilton of Bangour, who wrote "The Braes of Yarrow".

The idea of the idyllic pastoral life as described by Horace—who was fashionable in eighteenth-century Scotland—was enjoyed more by Hamilton than by any other eighteenth-century Scottish poet of note. Certainly Hamilton's correspondent, Allan Ramsay, was a hardworking Edinburgh man-about-town, and Robert Burns was very much a working tenant farmer who escaped from that grind by becoming an exciseman. An old Cambuslang lady, Mrs Turnbull, wife and mother of local

---

[2] We know that Hamilton of Gilbertfield's brother, John Hamilton, inherited Ladyland in 1690, but the Hamiltons had left Ladyland by 1710 when a Henry Moncrieff, who had a John Brisbane of Bishoptoun act as Commissioner for him, had some legal interest in the estate. Some few years before 1718 John Hamilton sold Ladyland to Alexander, ninth Earl of Eglintoun, who quickly sold it to William Cochrane of Edge, Lochwinnoch.

Having sold Ladyland, John Hamilton , brother of the poet of Gilbertfield, purchased an estate in the north of Ireland and through him we can make another link to two poets as he married "Margaret, daughter of Sir John Shaw, Bart. of Greenock, by Jean" who was the daughter of the covenanting poet Sir William Mure of Rowallan (1594-1657) whose great-uncle was the poet Alexander Montgomerie. The heir to John Hamilton sold the property in Ireland and purchased the estate of Craiglaw, in Wigtonshire, which was inherited by his brother, Charles Hamilton, Provost of Irvine for twelve years during the years 1758 to 1782.

The heir to the first Cochrane at Ladyland was another William and his son, yet another William, married, on 5th September 1815, Catherine Hamilton, a great-grand-daughter of the last Hamilton of Ladyland, and whose brother was William Hamilton of Craiglaw, a Lieutenant in the 10th Regiment of Dragoons, or Prince of Wales' own Regiment of Hussars. Through the marriage of Agnes, a daughter of William Cochrane and Catherine Hamilton, to William Patrick, Ladyland came to be owned by the Cochrane-Patrick family.

[3] Wilson, p.131. Duncan Glen, *A Nation in a Parish*, Edinburgh, 1995, pp.112-15. Also Duncan Glen, *A New History of Cambuslang,* Kirkcaldy, 1998.

doctors, John and Mungo Turnbull, reported around 1870 that her grandfather, who knew the poet, had described him as a "wee black-a-viced man, with brass buttons on his blue coat".[1]

We do not know when William Hamilton, the poet, came to Gilbertfield but an entry in the Old Parish Records of Cambuslang informs that in September 1705 there was born a "grandson to Archibald Hamilton of Gilbertfield" so it must have been after that date and before 1719 as Hamilton's first Epistle to Allan Ramsay is dated "Gilbertfield, June 26th, 1719". It may be that Hamilton came to Gilbertfield soon after 1705. I have found no entries in the Parish Records relating to children of Hamilton who was in his mid-forties when he came to Cambuslang. We know that, late in life, Hamilton was at Lettrick, on the slopes of Dechmont that face High Blantyre. Most of the lands of Lettrick were owned in the poet's time by the Duke of Hamilton.

Page from the edition of (?) 1719

ANSWER III.

A----- R-------- to W------ H-----------.

Edinburgh September 2d, 1719.

My Trusty TROJAN,

THY last ORATION ortholox,
Thy innocent auldfarran Jokes,
And sonsie Saw of Three, provokes
    Me ance again,
Tod Lawrie like to loose my Pocks,
    And pump my Brain.

BY a' your Letters I ha'e red,
I eithly scan the Man well bred,
And Sodger wha for Honour's Bed
    Has ventur'd bauld ;
Wha now to Youngsters leaves the Yed
    To 'tend his Fald.

THAT

The Mortality Bill and Mort-Cloth money records of the Parish of Cambuslang have three entries involving Hamilton. Two separate entries concern the death of his wife; both are dated 1748, Apr 26 and one of these names Lettrick, "Lieutenant Hamilton's Lady at Lettrick". The entry for Hamilton is dated 1751, May 24 and reads "Lieutenant Wm. Hamilton in Lettrick."—see frontispiece for a reproduction of this page. The two

---

[1] See Wilson p.132.

sums of money involved for Mrs Hamilton, burial with mort-cloth, are "0 . 3 . 8" and "—12" and the cost of the Mortality Bill and Mort-Cloth for Hamilton was "0 . 3 . 8"; this is a fair sum. Five entries below that for Hamilton is one dated Novr 13 which concerned my great-great-great-great-great grandparents and reads, "John Glen's child in Coats 0 . 0 . 7". I think it likely that Hamilton was buried in the kirkyard by the old church on Kirkhill, but it seems he has no memorial in the Parish where he wrote significant and influential literary works.

William Hamilton of Gilbertfield is known for four surviving works: (1) his mock-heroic animal fable, "The Last Dying Words of Bonny Heck", which was printed in part one of James Watson's pioneering *Choice Collection of Comic and Serious Scots Poems,* 1706; (2) three verse-epistles to Allan Ramsay, dated Gilbertfield, June 26th, July 24th and August 24th, all in 1719; (3) the song "Willie was a wanton wag" which Ramsay printed in his very popular anthology of Scots songs, *The Tea-Table Miscellany;* and (4) the work which, for almost two hundred years, made him a best-selling author—his modernised version of Blin Hary's great epic tale of *William Wallace.*

The first edition of Hamilton's very popular version of Hary's *Wallace* was printed in 1722 in Glasgow by William Duncan, in a foolscap 8vo edition (165mm) with the title-page in red and black. The

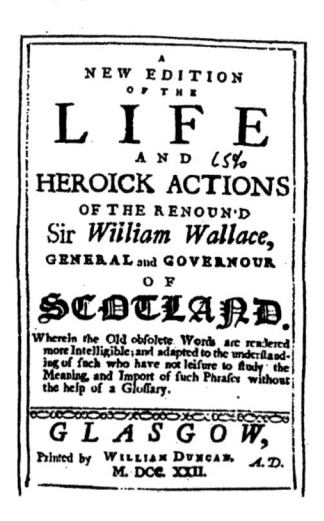

translator's dedication to the Duke of Hamilton is dated, Gilbertfield, 21st Sep. 1721. Until 1922 the Duke of Hamilton was the most important land-owner in the Parish, not selling off the considerable acreage of farmland that he rented out until that date, and often retaining the mineral rights.

In addition to the epistles printed here Hamilton also wrote, "An Epistle from William Hamilton to Allan Ramsay to make him a

Perewig"; this is dated, Gilbertfield 9th November 1719, and comprises 15 stanzas each of 9 lines; as was Ramsay's way, he printed this for sale as a broadsheet. Ramsay also wrote another epistle to Hamilton; this is "On the receiving the Compliment of a Barrel of Loch-Fyne Herrings from him 19th December, 1719". This epistle, which was published by Ramsay in an undated edition of probably early 1720, is in a ten-line stanza form which is also that of the poem "The Claith Merchant" which Ramsay printed in *The Ever-Green,* 1724.

In addition to "Willie was a wanton wag" Ramsay may have printed other songs by Hamilton in his *Tea-Table Miscellany*. Ramsay's aim was not to make individual poets known but, rather, to popularise Scottish poems and songs; to achieve that he had no hesitation in revising not only "old verses as have been done time out of mind" but also the new verses sent to him by living writers. In his "Preface" Ramsay acknowledged that for the first two volumes he had made verses for "about sixty" tunes and that "above thirty more were done by some ingenious young gentlemen, who were so well pleased with my undertaking, that they generously lent me their assistance; and to them the lovers of sense and music are obliged for some of the best songs in the collection." We cannot now know which verses were contributed by the "ingenious" Hamilton.

In a letter to George Thomson, editor and publisher of *A Select Collection of Original Scottish Airs,* Robert Burns, who knew far more than most about Scottish songs, wrote, "Since I am in the way of amending & abridging, let me recommend the following abridgement from a beautiful poem of Hamilton's to suit, 'Tak your auld cloak about ye'." Whilst Burns gave the words for a 44-line song, the song in the *Miscellany* has seven verses each of eight lines; this is the first,

> In winter when the rain rain'd cauld,
> And frost and snaw on ilka hill
> And Boreas, with his blasts sae bald,
> Was thret'ning a' our ky to kill;   ky, cows
> Then Bell, my wife, wha loves na strife,
> She said to me right hastily,
> Get up, goodman, save Cromy's life,
> And tak your auld cloak about ye.

In the same letter Burns continued, "For 'Willie was a wanton wag'—you have a song made on purpose, also by Hamilton, which you will find in Ramsay's Miscellany—beginning—'Willie, ne'er enquire what end'." In the *Miscellany* this song of four eight-line verses is entitled "Horace Book I Ode II [sic XI] To W.D.", who may be William Dalrymple of Cranstoun. The final verse ends,

17

> Then, Willie be a wanton wag,
> If ye wad please the lasses braw,
> At bridals then ye'll bear the brag,
> And carry ay the gree awa'.   *always the highest honours away*

Burns himself wrote a song, "Young Jockey was the blythest lad" which can also be related to these songs. Later in Ramsay's *Miscellany* are the words for "Willie was a wanton wag" which are more commonly ascribed to Hamilton, although not all editors have credited the poet of Gilbertfield with this lively version. We cannot be certain, but to deny this work to Hamilton is equivalent to those who, on poor evidence, deny "Auld Lang Syne" to Robert Burns. What we do know is that Hamilton signed his first verse epistle to Ramsay, "*Yours—wanton* WILLY".

In his *Illustrations of the Lyric Poetry and Music of Scotland*, 1853, William Stenhouse wrote that a version of this song was written about the beginning of the eighteenth century by "Mr Walkinshaw *of that ilk, near Paisley*". Stenhouse might have added that this is Mr William Walkinshaw, or W. W. He did add that a much older song "had previously been adapted to this lively tune". He also stated that "Ramsay, by a judicious alteration of one word in stanza first, another in stanza third, and one line in stanza sixth, improved this song very much." What seems likely, as T. F. Henderson noted in his *Scottish Vernacular Poetry: A Succinct History,* 1898, third revised edition 1910, is that Hamilton was influenced, directly or otherwise, by the English song, "O Willie was so blythe a Lad" (in Playford's *Choice Ayres*, 1650). Hamilton's version of the song begins,

> Willie was a wanton wag,
>   The blythest lad that e'er I saw:
> At bridals still he bore the brag,
>   And carried ay the gree awa':   *highest honours*
> His doublet was of Zetland shag,
>   And wow! but Willie he was braw,
> And at his shoulder hang a tag,
>   That pleas'ed the lasses best of a'.

2
GILBERTFIELD ESTATE AND CASTLE
and their surroundings

The estate of Gilbertfield may take its name from a member of the Moray family, Gilbert of Moray, Bishop of Caithness. About 1410, by when the barony of Drumsargart, with a castle at Hallside, had passed from the

Morays to the Douglases, Archibald, fourth Earl of Douglas, granted Gilbertfield by charter to John Park. From the 1550s to 1701 the lands of Gilbertfield were in the hands of the Cunningham family. A daughter of this family was the mother of Tobias Smollett, the novelist.

The castle at Gilbertfield was built, probably in 1607, by Sir Robert Cunningham, Knight, who died in 1628. Above each of the five dormer windows there were monograms resembling a letter C with a W within it. In his *History of Cambuslang,* 1929, James Wilson noted that over each of these was "a coronet standing in relief. The suggestion follows that this combination represents a person of higher rank than a baronet. Possibly that person was William Cunningham, Earl of Glencairn, nevertheless the Gilbertfield Cunninghams are not mentioned in any account of the Glencairn family."[1] On the east wall there was the date 1607 above a monogram with the letters R.C; the west and south walls also had monograms—none of these was surmounted by a coronet.

Four lairds on from Sir Robert Cunningham, in June 1701, Robert Cunningham sold the lands of Gilbertfield to Archibald Hamilton, minister of Cambuslang, and a grandson of Andrew Hamilton, laird of Westburn, and nephew of Gabriel Hamilton, also of Westburn, whose wife was Margaret Cunningham, very probably a granddaughter of the builder of the castle. In 1702 Rev. Hamilton sold Gilbertfield, with Overton and Bellhouseside, to his cousin Archibald Hamilton of Carmunnock who was also to become laird of Westburn, and lived till about 1733 when he was succeeded at Westburn by his son Gabriel Hamilton who died in 1761. The Westburn estate bordered the Clyde near where the river was fordable, and is today crossed by Clydeford Road bridge, the main road out of Cambuslang going past Carmyle to Junction 2 of the M74. Westburn House stood in what is today Cambuslang Golf Club, but all that remains is the doocot.

It was in 1827 that the trustees of the late Adam Graham of Craigallian bought the lands of Westburn, Gilbertfield, parts of Bellhouseside and 5 acres of the Kirkland, and in 1839 John Graham took the Duke of Hamilton to court over the mineral rights of Gilbertfield, Overton and Bellhouseside. When the colliery that stood almost opposite the gasworks on Hamilton Road was closed in 1906 it was owned by A. G. Barns Graham, who had served as Convener of the County. In November 1966 Robert Taylor, who had been farming near Milngavie, came to Gilbertfield Farm as a tenant of Barns Graham. Following the storm of 1968, Barns Graham sold the lands of Gilbertfield, with farm buildings and the castle, to Mr Taylor who still owns the property.

---

[1] Wilson, page 133.

When Rev Archibald Hamilton was ordained minister at Cambuslang in June 1688 the times were troubled. King James VII was deposed and replaced by William of Orange and Queen Mary early in 1689 and the long Episcopal years of what Presbyterian historians accurately term "The Killing Times" were at an end although, when Hamilton was ordained, the legal establishment of Presbyterianism was still two years away. The Highland rising on behalf of James VII, led by John Graham of Claverhouse, Viscount Dundee, achieved a notable victory over the government forces at Killiecrankie in July 1689 but the death of Dundee meant that the Royalist cause lacked an inspirational leader. The covenanters of Lowland Cambuslang would have rejoiced at the failure of the Royalist campaign and, no doubt, shown little sympathy for the Macdonalds massacred at Glencoe on the night of 13th February 1692 by soldiers of King William's government.

Rev Archibald Hamilton, who would be living in a church house whilst the poet was in his old castle-tower home, died in Cambuslang on 3rd January 1725, "in the 63rd year of his age and the 35th of his ministry". This lairdly minister seems to have been interested in literature and so, in August 1719, would have been genuinely pleased to be mentioned in Hamilton's Epistle III to Allan Ramsay,

> I shaw'd it to our Parish Priest
> Wha was as blyth as gi'm a Feast.
> He says, "Thou may had up thy Creest,
>   And craw fu' crouse

Kirkhill, Cambuslang, c. 1884, after a sketch by A. K. Brown.

The modern church was built in 1841. The building cost near enough £3,300 about half of which was paid by the tenth Duke of Hamilton. The next most generous contributor was John Graham of Westburn, Gilbertfield etc.

For those coming to Cambuslang to see Gilbertfield Castle, the first point of reference is the elegant spire of the Parish Church; from the church Cairns Road, running alongside the Public Park within which are the preaching braes of the great religious revival of 1742, leads into Gilbertfield Road and the castle-tower stands in fields beyond Gilbertfield Farm. For most of this century Dechmont Hill has been owned by the Ministry of Defence and its slopes used as a rifle range, which means that there has been limited access for hillwalkers. No soldiers have been seen on the hill in recent months and it *could be* that the government is considering selling the properties it owns hereabouts.

Gilbertfield is one of the buildings described by MacGibbon and Ross in volume 2 of their *The Castellated and Domestic Architecture of Scotland,* 1887-92, and they not only printed drawings that gave views of the tower from the North-West and the South-East (which I reproduce on pages 23 and 29) but also plans of the ground and first floors, which I also print here. They also recognised the tower's "retired position on the lower slopes of Dechmont Hill" and that Gilbertfield stands high with a fine view over "the Vale of Clyde". They also wrote of it having a "commanding and venerable aspect" and, despite the collapse of walls

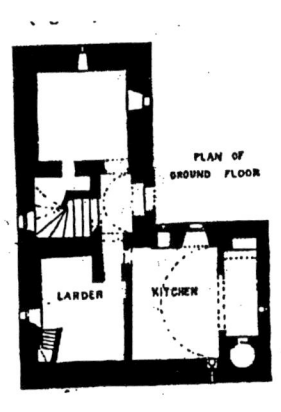

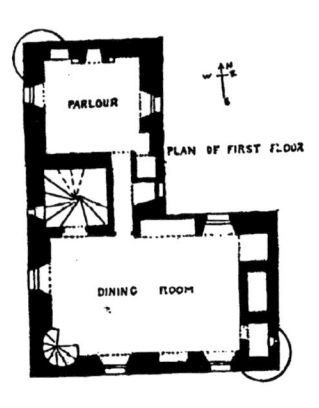

and roofs, it remains an impressive structure. The description given by MacGibbon and Ross was incorporated by George Henderson and J. Jeffrey Waddell into their excellent *By Bothwell Banks*, 1904.[1] Indeed Waddell takes several fine phrases from the earlier writers into what is one of the few reasonably detailed descriptions of Gilbertfield,

> The castle is situated near the base of Dechmont Hill, about a mile and a half from Newton and two miles from Uddingston. It is L shaped on plan and is four storeys high. The entrance doorway, which is lintelled, is in

---

[1] J. Jeffrey Waddell had architectural knowledge and so was well qualified to describe the castle. Many Cambuslang children were entertained by the travelling children's theatre of Bertha Waddell, daughter of Mr Waddell. I can well remember, at West Coats School in the 1940s, the announcement of "Item Number One".

the angle, and is commanded by a shot-hole from the kitchen and also from above. There has been a carved panel immediately above the lintel of the door. The castle is a very good example of the period of transition from the more ancient keep to the modern mansion. The windows, especially on the ground floor, are small, and all are barred with iron. The walls are about 3ft. 4in. thick. Although manifestly not built to withstand a regular siege, it is quite evident from what we see of its construction that it could have given a hostile party a very warm reception. But this does not interfere with its picturesqueness. It is very dignified in appearance, yet at the same time quaint and homely, the little corner turrets and crow-stepped gables, all well-proportioned, uniting to give the whole building a very pleasing outline.

Entering into the interior through the door in the angle referred to, we again note in passing how the doorway could have been commanded by the fire of the inmates, one of the loopholes indeed being so near the entrance as to make it absolutely impossible for any hostile person to damage or even to approach the door. On the ground floor are the kitchen, larder, and a room which may have been an armoury. These rooms and the entrance lobby are barrel-vaulted, the height being about 10ft. 8in. The kitchen fireplace is large, measuring 14ft. by 5ft., and has a fine round arch with an ingle seat at one end and an oven at the other. A stone sink with a drain occupies a recess in the wall. Large rusty iron cleeks still remain in the ceiling, testifying to a lavish hospitality long since passed away. There is a small service-stair from the larder to the dining-room, which is immediately overhead. This is a large room, 27ft. by 17ft., with a ceiling 14ft. 3in. high. It had a large fire-place which, however, has been contracted in modern times.

Proceeding along a short passage a smaller room is reached. This is called "Queen Mary's Room," as she is said to have slept here. Unfortunately for this story the date on the dormer already referred to is some twenty years after Mary's execution, and while it might still be maintained that the dated portion represented a later addition to the castle, it is more than likely that we must relegate this tradition to a place in the great mass of legendary history which a pitying interest in Mary's sad career has gathered round her name. In the thickness of this parlour wall a small closet with a loop-hole commands the entrance, whence in the good old days the master of the house could give rather a sharp welcome to any hostile intruder on his privacy. The second floor has been modernised, but has been originally used as bedrooms only. The attic floor is similar, with the addition of two very fine little oriels. These, while they may have been used by the lady of the house as bowers, could also be utilised to command the base of the walls; but taken by themselves there is certainly nothing half so charming in the modern villa as this old Scottish feature. In elevation these features harmonise with the crow-stepped gables, and together with the dormer windows, which are ornamented with crescent finials, monograms, dates, etc., give character to the castle. The walls are of grey sandstone, rough cast in places; the flooring-joists and rafters are of oak (jointed with oak pins), and the slats are also fixed with oak trenails. The ridge is of sandstone.

From MacGibbon and Ross, Gilbertfield from the North-West

It is only recently that there has been an upsurge in the restoration of Scottish castle-towers and the tower at Gilbertfield has been falling further into ruin throughout this century. In 1929, Dr James Wilson, revealing untypical commitment and lyricism, wrote, "On the northern slopes of Dechmont, Gilbertfield Castle stands isolated and silent. Trees, gardens, stables, and people are gone; only an almost roofless ruin remains, a skeleton of something that was elegant and strong, something that was medieval and modern, something that is rich in human and literary associations. It is now given over to the beasts of the field and the birds of the air." In volume 3, "South West Scotland", of his *The Fortified House in Scotland,* 1962, Nigel Tranter wrote, "Within the last twenty years the entire east gable of the main block has collapsed."

The view that William Hamilton had from the turret windows of Gilbertfield was both beautiful and extensive and when he rode to the summit of Dechmont he could enjoy a prospect that was very well described in the early 1790s by Rev Dr James Meek who wrote the description of the parish of Cambuslang for *The Statistical Account of Scotland,* 1793, and saw his parish as being "Distinguished by its beautiful scenery, and from the top of Dichmount, there is certainly one of the finest inland prospects in Scotland."

It cannot have been too long after the poet left Gilbertfield that the castle-tower was left to begin its slow movement towards ruin. Certainly by the 1830s John Struthers, poet of East Kilbride and Dechmont Hill, was able to describe it as an uninhabited ruin and address Hamilton,

> Here, Gilbertfield! . . .
> Peace to thy spirit! On my ear
> Even the light summer-breeze sounds drear
> Around thy ruin'd castle-walls,
> And through thy lone, deserted halls,
> Where Cheerfulness should laughing stray,
> The Muses and the Graces play.

In the 1790s John Struthers returned to his native village of East Kilbride to live with his wife at Nethermains on the East Kilbride to Hamilton road and, some sixty years later, he gave a lyrical description of the view from his cottage. The New Town of East Kilbride has been built on much good farm land but what Struthers saw in the 1790s was known not only to Hamilton of Gilbertfield but also to those who knew the lands around East Kilbride and Dechmont through the first forty-five years of this century. Nethermains cottage stood a little to the east of Long Calderwood and it enjoyed, wrote Struthers,

> one of the most lovely landscapes that could be imagined, embracing part of the lands of Long Calderwood, the finely cultivated fields of Nerston, the Turnley, Crookedshiel and Letterick Hills; the western portion of the beautiful pastoral hill of Dychmont, and in the distance the fells of the Lennox, Ben Lomond, with the greater number of his gigantic brethren, the sky-propping family of the Bens. A walk of a few hundred yards along the road to the eastward brings the traveller to the head of the Cadgerloan brae, whence is spread out before him one of the most lovely inland landscapes to be met with in Scotland. At his feet stands Crossbasket in a deep and richly wooded dell of the Calder, extending, by the mansion house of Greenhall, all the way down to Millheugh; having on the right the broom-clad braes of Basket, the spreading woods of Achentibber, with the parish and kirktown of Blantyre; on the left the eastern peak with the fine house of Dychmont, the splendid fields of Flemington and the two Lettericks, with the hoary ruins and gorgeous woods of Bothwell Castle; while in the distance expand before him part of the parish of Campsie, Kirkintilloch, Kilsyth, the two Monklands, with the towns of Airdrie and Coatbridge, Cumbernauld, Bertram, Shotts, Cambusnethan, and Dalziel; terminating in the towering tops of the Pentlands, the glorious range of the green Ochils, and the far distant hills of the kingdom of Fife.
>
> In addition to all this, the subject of this memoir had, from Sir William Maxwell, the liberty of all the avenues around the house, and through the charming woods and sequestered dells of Calderwood, which

though then far from the state of tasteful beauty and chastened grandeur to which they have now been brought by the present proprietor of the same name, were yet, perhaps, in the exuberant prodigality of unrestrained nature, fitted to inspire the mind with a still higher feeling of wild magnificence and savage sublimity.

3
ALLAN RAMSAY (1684-1758)
of Edinburgh

Born on 15th October 1684[2] in the lead-mining village of Leadhills in Lanarkshire, Allan Ramsay went, probably in the first year of the eighteenth century, to Edinburgh to become an apprentice to a wigmaker. He did enrol as a master wigmaker, probably with premises in the Grassmarket, but gradually he gave up this trade, gravitating into the world of letters as a popular poet and an influential and patriotic editor, publisher and bookseller. The Easy Club, which he helped to found in 1712, gave patriots such as Ramsay a forum for readings and much talk. From 1718 his poems were, to quote from their title-pages, published by "the Author at the *Mercury,* opposite to Niddry's Wynd". This shop was on the High Street, a little downhill from the Tron Kirk; later Ramsay moved to premises "at the East End of the Luckenbooths" close by the

Portrait frontispiece from the subscribers' edition of Allan Ramsay's *Poems,* 1721.

High Kirk of St Giles. The site of this centrally-placed shop was later occupied by William Creech, who published two editions of the poems of Robert Burns, in 1787 and a two-volume edition of 1793. Following the publication of the 1787 edition, Burns, on the advice of Henry

---

[2] Traditionally the year of Ramsay's birth is 1685 but Alexander Manson Kinghorn and Alexander Law, editors of volumes III to VI of the Scottish Text Society's edition of Ramsay's poems, favour 1684.

Mackenzie, author of the sentimental novel, *A Man of Feeling,* sold the copyright of *Poems Chiefly in the Scottish Dialect* to Creech for 100 guineas. As Michael Schmidt wrote in his "Note on the Text" of a new edition, 1999, of Burns's first edition, "It was a serious mistake, and like all such mistakes dictated by necessity rather than prudence."

At his shop in the Luckenbooths Ramsay established a circulating library, perhaps the first in Britain. Even more ambitiously, he opened a theatre in Carrubber's Close but a London Act of 1737 forbidding the performance of plays for gain outside London gave the Edinburgh Presbytery the means to close it down. As an anthologist of Scottish poems, Ramsay followed the example of the equally-patriotic James Watson whose *A Choice Collection of Comic and Serious Scots Poems both Ancient and Modern* was published in three parts in 1706, 1709 and 1711. The title-page of the second edition of Part 1 of Watson's anthology informs that it was "Printed by James Watson, and Sold at his Shop, next door to the *Red-Lyon,* opposite to the *Lucken-Booths,* 1713", opposite where Ramsay and Creech were to have their shops.

Creech's shop in a high building in the Luckenbooths close to the walls of St Giles.

The Luckenbooths were locked shops as opposed to the open stalls. In the narrow passageway between the shops and the wall of the church there were, from the sixteenth century, between the buttresses of the church, crowded rows of tiny open stalls known as the krames, many of which sold toys; to Lord Cockburn in the nineteenth century these were, "the paradise of childhood". It was said that Ramsay's shop became the "Hub of the Universe" and certainly all manner of men foregathered there, as they continued to do when Creech was there. The *Epistles* of Hamilton and Ramsay were bought in these premises as, in Creech's time, were the works of Burns. Creech had the Edinburgh edition of Burns's poems printed by William Smellie who had his premises in Anchor Close which runs from the north side of the High Street down to Cockburn Street. In this Close stood Dawney Douglas's Anchor Tavern where the Crochallon Fencibles met. It was Smellie who took Burns to this somewhat disreputable club.

In gathering verses for Scots songs into his *The Tea-Table Miscellany* Ramsay achieved a bestseller. The first edition is dated 1723, and there were twelve reprints during Ramsay's lifetime and twenty-four during the eighteenth century; that printed in Perth in 1793 is described as the eighteenth.

In contrast to this best-seller, in Ramsay's lifetime there was only one edition of his *The Ever Green,* first published in 1724. This anthology is of major importance as Ramsay printed work by early poets whose poems had been preserved by George Bannatyne, Edinburgh merchant, in his personal manuscript anthology, perhaps completed in 1568. Walter Scott was not exaggerating too excessively when he wrote of the young Bannatyne's "courageous energy to form and execute the plan of saving the literature of a nation". Ramsay was loaned this priceless manuscript, and his own anthology was important in making the poetry of the old makars, saved by Bannatyne, available to his contemporaries.

Ramsay published his own poems in many forms; broadsheets, pamphlets and collections in which he "gathered up" poems for various issues and editions, but more formally collected subscribers' editions, with the scholarly Thomas Ruddiman acting as printer, were published in 1721 and 1728. Ramsay published his pastoral play, *The Gentle Shepherd,* in 1725 and in 1728 he was persuaded to make a ballad-opera version which became very popular. Allan Ramsay may not have written great poetry but he did alter the course of Scottish literature—and so, also, the history of Scotland.

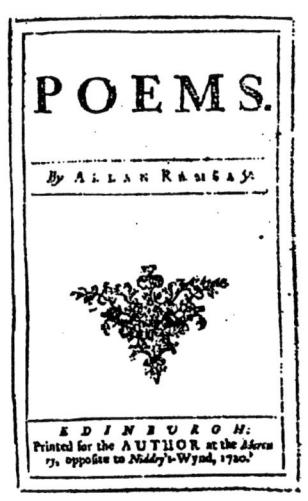

A fine statue of Ramsay stands in Edinburgh above the very popular cuckoo clock in Princes Street Gardens, at the foot of The Mound; high above, immediately below the Castle, stands the octagonal house that Ramsay built for his years of retirement. It is known as the Goose-Pie,

and that seems apt for this cheerful and very busy man whom I can readily envisage bustling up the High Street to Castlehill and what is today Ramsay Garden. During the Jacobite occupation of Edinburgh in the 1745 rebellion Allan Ramsay diplomatically retreated to Penicuik and the Jacobites took his "Goose-Pie" house from which they fired on the sentries at the Castle, which remained in the hands of the Government. No Scot has worked harder or more creatively for his country than Allan Ramsay. He gave us a little witty self-portrait in his "An Epistle to Mr James Arbuckle of Belfast", dated Edinburgh, January 1719,

Imprimis then, for tallness I	In the first place
Am five foot and four inches high:	
A black-a-viced snod dapper fallow,	neat, trim
Nor lean, nor overlaid wi' tallow.	
With phiz of a Morocco cut,	

Allan Ramsay was successful and famous; he was as much a role model as is Stephen Hendry, seven times snooker world champion. These men provided personal examples that showed what was achievable; they were not an aspect of a historic imperative. In this century the personal example of Hugh MacDiarmid encouraged many other poets to write in Scots and to have high poetic ambitions. The poets may give themselves supporting cultural and personal structures but again that is personal to both great and minor poets. It was helpful for MacDiarmid to envisage a Scottish Renaissance, and that concept changed the way his contemporaries viewed the world they were writing in; but MacDiarmid wrote what was born in him to write, and so also did those who were able to learn from him without being stifled, suffocated and overwhelmed by his achievements. Similarly, we may doubt that Alexander Montgomerie's work was influenced very much by James VI's manifesto for a new Scottish poetry. This is not to deny the importance of the King's patronage, or the need for modern poets to be given the encouragement of publication. Both the flitting of King James VI to London and the Union of the Scottish and English Parliaments in 1707 diminished Scottish cultural confidence. The pro-Union *literati,* as they liked to call themselves, of Edinburgh revealed what Australians today call "cultural cringe", the willing acceptance of inferiority towards another country, be it England or the USA. In their poetry neither Hamilton nor Ramsay impose any cringe onto us and by writing his version of Blin Hary's *Wallace* within the sturdy walls of Gilbertfield castle-tower Hamilton made a significant contribution to keeping alive the idea of a culturally independent Scotland.

From MacGibbon and Ross, Gilbertfield from the South-East

4

THE VERSE FORM OF THE EPISTLES OF HAMILTON AND RAMSAY,
AND THEIR PLACE WITHIN THE SCOTTISH LITERARY TRADITION

William Hamilton, the poet of Cambuslang's Gilbertfield, would be important in the history of Scottish poetry if he had written only "The Last Dying Words of Bonny Heck". In this context the verse form is more important than the poem although only good poems encourage emulation of their form. Allan Ramsay immediately recognised this as a form very suited to his own work, including the poems where he used a mode of very-aware burlesque which could send up the pompous and over-serious. In using the form for a comic, mock elegy for an animal, Hamilton both began a fashion and continued an old tradition.

As a successful poet, editor, publisher and bookseller Allan Ramsay gave literary models to his successors, including the verse forms of "Chrystis Kirk on the Grene", possibly written about 1500, and "The Cherrie and the Slae" by Alexander Montgomerie (c.1545-c.1610). Here I am interested in the verse form that Hamilton of Gilbertfield used for his "The Last Dying Words of Bonny Heck" and also for his "Familiar Epistles" which he sent from Gilbertfield to Allan Ramsay in Edinburgh. Hamilton was seen by T. F. Henderson as "the main link in the succession between the Sempills and Ramsay". The influential work is Robert Sempill's, "The Life and Death of the Piper of Kilbarchan", or "The Epitaph of Habbie Simson" written about 1640.

> Kilbarchan now may say alas!
> For she hath lost her game and grace,
> Both *Trixie* and *The Maiden Trace;*
>   But what remead?
> For no man can supply his place:
>   Hab Simson's dead.
>
> Now who shall we play *The Daw it Dawis,*
> Or *Hunt's Up*, when the cock he craws?
> Or who can for our kirk-town cause
>   Stand us in stead?
> On bagpipes now nobody blaws
>   Sen Habbie's dead.

In one of his verse-epistles to Hamilton of Gilbertfield, Ramsay referred to this stanza as "Standart Habbie" and he popularised its use.

The verse form that was used for the early work "Chrystis Kirk on the Grene" was, before Sempill, Hamilton and Ramsay, even more popular than "Standart Habbie". This stanza, with a complicated rhyme structure, was much used for poems that celebrated exuberant festivals, and these poems have been described as belonging to the "peasant brawl" tradition of Scottish poetry. The "jingling" effect of the rhyme scheme of the sixteenth-century "Chrystis Kirk on the Grene" was toned down in the eighteenth century, but this light-hearted quality is also in the rhymes and flow of the shorter "Standart Habbie" stanza, and Hamilton and Ramsay tended to heighten rather than subdue this characteristic of popular Scots verse. Even the title of Hamilton's "The Last Dying Words of Bonny Heck, A Famous Grey-Hound in the Shire of Fife" is part of the mock-seriousness of the poem which begins with Hamilton burlesqueing the high seriousness of the heroic and doughty deeds related in Blin Hary's *Wallace* which Hamilton held in very high regard as his popular version of the poem shows,

> Alas, alas, quo' bonny *Heck*,
> On former Days when I reflect!
> I was a Dog much in Respect
>   For doughty Deed:
> But now I must hing by the Neck
>   Without Remeed.
>
> O fy, Sirs, for black burning Shame,
> Ye'll bring a Blunder on your Name!
> Pray tell me wherein I'm to blame?
>   Is't in Effect,
> Because I'm Criple, Auld and Lame?
>   Quo' bony *Heck*.

Unlike many post-Burns poets, Allan Ramsay knew that Scottish poets before Sempill used this old six-line stanza. In his reply Hamilton wishes he could be as "gabby" or talkative as Ramsay or Habbie, and the suitability of the form for a colloquial poetry now seems to be obvious. That said, the use made of the stanza by Alexander Scott (c.1515-c.1584), poet of the courts of James VI and Mary, Queen of Scots, was less light-hearted, as this verse from his "A Complaint Against Cupid" shows,

What is thy manrent bot mischief,	thy homage paid to a superior
Sturt, anger, grunching, ire, and grief,	Trouble, anger, grumbling
Evil life, and langour but releif	
Of woundis wan,	dire
Displeasure, pain, and hie repreif	reproof
Of God and man?	

In using this old form for verse-epistles Hamilton and Ramsay gave it a new purpose and their lively and inventive use of the form impressed Robert Fergusson (1750-74), and Robert Burns acknowledged his debt to a trio of his predecessors in his epistle "To William Simson, Ochiltree", written in May 1785,

> My senses wad be in a creel,   *in a basket (to be crazed)*
> Should I but dare a *hope* to speel,   *climb*
> Wi Allan, or wi' Gilbertfield,
>   The braes o' fame;
> Or Fergusson, the writer-chiel,   *young writer fellow*
>   A deathless name.

In their verse-epistles Hamilton and Ramsay aimed to be familiar, friendly and light yet inventive, displaying a delight in language and amused by their own literary conceits. They could smile confidently at those who were unable to recognise the mode within which they were writing. We can readily see that this was truly a word game in which the poets took pleasure in employing, and displaying to each other, wit and technical skill. Well might Robert Burns, in a letter of April 1786 to Robert Aiken, write of "the famous Ramsay of jingling memory" when quoting the first line of the first verse of Ramsay's "Answer" to Hamilton's second Epistle,

> Set out the burnt side of your shin,[1]
> For pride in poets is nae sin,
> Glory's the prize for which they rin,
>   And fame's their jo;
> And wha blaws best the horn shall win:
>   And wharefor no?

Wit is, of course, in the ear of the reader, and the wit of Ramsay's epistles has been regarded as not only dated but also too familar, too hamespun. Yet, as Sydney Goodsir Smith excellently wrote, when linking Robert Fergusson's "Braid Claith", which is also in "Standart Habbie", to the Byron of "Beppo" and "Donny Johnny", the wit "is not so much in the thought as in the rhyme itself". "Beppo" has been well described as "a curtain-raiser" for *Don Juan* which, like so many poems in "Standart Habbie", is full of such word fun. Sydney Goodsir Smith compared two lines by Byron with a verse from Burns's "Address to the Deil",

> What men call gallantry, and gods adultery,
> Is much more common where the climate's sultry.

---

[1] Ramsay glossed: "As if one would say, walk stately with your toes out. An expression used when we bid a person (merrily) look brisk"

> Then you, ye auld, snick-drawing dog!
> Ye cam to Paradise incog.
> An' play'd on man a cursed brogue,
> > (Black be your fa'!)
> An' gied the infant warld a shog,   *shock, jog*
> > 'Maist ruin'd a'.

Goodsir Smith could have added that his own poetry, especially the masterly *Under the Eildon Tree,* 1948, is also enriched by similar wit as, indeed, is the poetry of Hugh MacDiarmid.

One of the best of Ramsay's elegies within this tradition of conversational and familiar poems is "Elegy on Lucky Wood in the Canongate, May 1717",

> She gae'd as fait as a new prin,
> And kept her housie snod and been;   *neat*
> Her peuther glanc'd upo' your een   *pewter eyes*
> > Like siller plate;
> She was a donsie wife and clean,   *clean little person*
> > Without debate.

Robert Fergusson (1750-74) certainly learned much from the works of Hamilton and Ramsay but, from his earliest poems in Scots, he used the "Standart Habbie" stanza with more seriousness than any of his eighteenth-century predecessors. His contribution to the elegiac tradition written in the stanza includes an "Elegy, On the Death of Mr David Gregory, late Professor of Mathematics in the University of St Andrews". This has been seen as the first poem in "Standart Habbie" to have a "respectable" person for its subject. Although unlikely, this could be a very early poem written by Ferguson when he was a teenage student in St Andrews. The short final line of each verse, which follows an exaggerated detailing of the Professor's many claims to fame as a mathematician, is, with the exception of the final verse, either following Robert Sempill on the death of Habbie Simson, "Sin Gregory's dead", or "But now he's dead". The elegy remains a mock one, yet there is an extra dimension within this amusing poem; we are aware that this was a man who lived and taught in St Andrews and that now he is very much "dead". The cumulative effect of verse after verse is important, but this one may hint at what Fergusson achieved with a verse form that was to be degraded by generations of local rhymsters who imitated Burns,

> In algebra weel skill'd he was,
> An' kent fu' well proportion's laws;
> He cou'd make clear baith B's and A's
> > Wi his lang head;
> Rin owre surd roots, but cracks or flaws;
> > But now he's dead.

Amongst other of Fergusson's poems written in this form are "Elegy, On the Death of Scots Music", "Braid Claith", and "The Tron Kirk Bell" which gives a new dimension to the old flyting tradition of hurling formalised abuse at an adversary,

Wanwordy, crazy, dinsome thing,	worthless
As e'er fram'd to jow or ring,	toll
What gar'd them sic in steeple hing	caused such
They ken themsel'	know
But weel wat I coudna bring	well know
War sounds frae hell.	worse

As a true "makar", skilled in verse forms, Fergusson had learned from English Augustan formalism, as his juxtaposition of this "foreign" style with his Scots in "Elegy, on the Death of Scots Music" reveals. Where Ramsay, whom Fergusson echoes in some phrases, used the "Standart Habbie" stanza for rambunctious mock elegies, Fergusson used it to express an irony as subtle as that heard in Augustan English writing, or polite Johnsonian conversation of that time,

Mourn ilka nymph and ilka swain,	every
Ilk sunny hill and dowie glen;	gloomy
Let weeping streams and Naiads drain	
Their fountain head;	
Let echo swell the dolefu' strain,	
Since music's dead.	

Of course, Burns used this stanza beyond equal, and this very old form even became known to the rhymsters who imitated the style and verse forms of his poems as the "Burns stanza".

We can thank William Hamilton of Gilbertfield not only for reviving the "Standart Habbie" stanza in his own mock elegy "Bonny Heck", but also for continuing a tradition of animal poems that goes back to the *Fables* of Robert Henrysoun (c.1420-c.1490). This comic tradition of mock testaments spoken by dying animals was exploited by Robert Burns in, for example, "The Death and Dying Words of Poor Mailie". This is an early poem, not in "Standart Habbie" but in polished octosyllables, which was written at Lochlea farm, near Tarbolton, which Burns's father leased from 1777 and the family left in 1784. Although an occasional piece, which was written to describe an amusing incident at Lochlea farm, this poem was certainly worthy of inclusion in Burns's first volume, *Poems Chiefly in the Scottish Dialect,* the Kilmarnock edition of July 1786. A later poem, which was also printed in the Kilmarnock edition, is "Poor Mailie's Elegy", and this is a direct descendant of "The Life and Death of Habbie Simson" and poems by Hamilton, Ramsay and Fergusson,

> Thro' a' the town she trotted by him;
> A lang half-mile she would descry him;
> Wi' kindly bleat, when she did spy him,
>   She ran wi' speed:
> A friend mair faithfu' ne'er came nigh him,
>   Than *Mailie* dead.

Burns raised the "Standart Habbie" stanza to unequalled heights in poem after poem including the unequalled "Holy Willie's Prayer". Willie's monstrous self-regarding prayer moves to a climax that is all the more satirical for sounding so authentic, so sonorously religious, with the genius of Burns clearly seen in his merging of "grace & gear" in one fluent and natural-seeming phrase,

> But Lord; remember me and mine
> Wi' mercies temporal & divine!
> That I for grace & gear may shine,   *grace and wealth*
>   Excell'd by nane!
> And a' the glory shall be thine!
>   Amen! Amen!

Burns wrote "Tam o' Shanter" for Captain Grose, an antiquarian, and there is a dazzlingly bright poem, "On the Late Captain Grose's Peregrinations thro' Scotland, collecting the Antiquities of that Kingdom". The full title is important in setting the ironical but friendly tone of Burns's poem; a masterpiece of the "Standart Habbie" tradition,

> Hear, Land o' Cakes, and brither Scots,
> Frae Maidenkirk to Johny Groats!—
> If there's a hole in a' your coats,
>   I rede you tent it: *advise you look to it*
> A chield's amang you, taking notes,   *fellow*
>   And, faith, he'll prent it.

As used by the nineteenth-century rhymesters who imitated Burns, the "Habbie" stanza became a vehicle for sentimental, couthy, and worthless verse. A sad decline for a stanza used by the Provençal troubadours, great medieval Scots makars, and passed via Sempill to Hamilton, Ramsay, Fergusson and Burns. Robert Louis Stevenson did restore some dignity to the stanza, and in this century Robert Garioch revived it with considerable panache, as even one verse from his "To Robert Fergusson" shows,

> And what a knack ye had o screivin   *writing*
> in caller verse yon wroth o livin,   *fresh*
> your wee stane warld o fechtin, thievin,
>   drinkin and swinkin,   *working*
> wi muckle fun and puckle grievin   *much, little*
>   and fowth o thinkin.   *plenty*

It is regrettable that neither John Wilson (1720-89), author of *Clyde*, 1803 and 1859, nor John Struthers (1776-1853), author of *Dychmont*, 1836, was able to learn from the example of William Hamilton of Gilbertfield, although Struthers did use the stanza in early poems in Scots and in the excessively literary "To the Blackbird".

Here I emphasise the importance of verses by William Hamilton of Gilbertfield but for about a century he was famous not as a poet but for his adaptation of Blin Hary's great epic poem on William Wallace. Hary (c.1440-92) wrote his masterpiece of Scottish patriot pride about 1477 and by the Act of Union of 1707 it had been printed in many editions. The Union encouraged those with ambitions for themselves, or their children, to succeed in London, or through London influence, to reject the old Scottish traditions, including that of Scottish literature. Others, including Allan Ramsay, responded to the Union by working to advance Scottish literature, and his publications encouraged an upsurge of patriotism. So it was that Hamilton of Gilbertfield set about making a version of Hary's *Wallace* that could be more easily read by his contemporaries than Hary's great original. Hamilton's version was published in 1722 and became a bestseller, going through by 1859 as many editions as Hary's original work. It says something about Victorian and twentieth-century Scotland, that from that edition Hamilton's work was not reprinted until 1998 when Luath Press published a very well-printed edition with a stimulating introduction by Elspeth King.

As Neil MacCallum writes in his essay, modern critics have tended to patronise Hamilton and "dismiss him as an obscure, if interesting, footnote in the literary history of Scotland". His version of Blin Hary's *Wallace* has been particularly harshly criticised in this twentieth century but, as the short extract I have selected for printing here shows, the popularity of his work was not undeserved.

Interest in William Wallace has been stimulated by the film *Braveheart* but this national hero has never been out of favour with the people of Scotland. In her Introduction to the Luath edition, Elspeth King wrote of Blin Hary's *Wallace*,

> No other single work of literature in Scotland has had such an influence on the map makers and no work of fiction could achieve this. The naming of places after Wallace's deeds was reinforced by Hanilton's popular edition, when, armed with a copy, the blacksmiths, ploughmen, weavers and washerwomen actively sought in their particular localities the oak where Wallace sheltered, the stone around which he gathered his troops, the road along which he marched, and the places where he gave battle. . . Memories of Wallace were invested in and entrusted to the natural features of the land. R. B. Cunninghame Graham articulated this when he wrote

> Wallace made Scotland. He is Scotland; he is the symbol of all that is best and purest and truest and most heroic in our national life. You cannot figure to yourself Scotland without Wallace. So long as grass grows green or water runs, whilst the mist curls through the corries of the hills, the name of Wallace will live.

It was Hamilton's *Wallace* which enabled the name of Wallace to live in this way.

Before Burns, Hary's *Wallace* was one of two books, with the poems of Sir David Lyndsay (1486-1555) the other, that challenged the Bible for space on the bookshelves of literate Scots. In the revolutionary years of the eighteenth century William Wallace became one of the symbols for freedom. William Wordsworth certainly so regarded the Scottish patriot, and so did Robert Burns. In September 1793, in a letter to George Thomson, publisher of *A Selected Collection of Original Scottish Airs, 1793-1818*, Burns acknowledged that he had "borrowed" the last stanza of "Scots Wha Hae" "from the common Stall edition of Wallace,—'A false usurper sinks in ev'ry foe,/ And Liberty returns with every blow'. A couplet worthy of Homer." The lines are from Book 6, Chapter 2, of Hamilton's version of Hary's *Wallace* which tells the story of the bloody Battle of Biggar. In his very famous autobiographical letter to Dr Moore Burns wrote,

> The first two books that I ever read in private, and which gave me more pleasure than any two books I ever read again, were, the life of Hannibal and the history of Sir William Wallace. Hannibal gave my young ideas such a turn that I used to strut in raptures up and down after the recruiting drum and bagpipe, and wish myself tall enough to be a soldier; while the story of Wallace poured a Scottish prejudice in my veins which will boil along there till the floodgates of life shut in eternal rest.

The final verse of "Scots Wha Hae" is,

> Lay the proud usurpers low!
> Tyrants fall in every foe!
> Liberty in every blow! —
> Let us do, or die!

Today, with our awareness of two world wars and "tribal" warfare continuing across continents, we may not like the violence of Hary's account of the battle or be comfortable with the nationalistic tone of "Scots Wha Hae". Also, we may be fortunate and not to have to "do, or die", but we can peacefully appreciate and nurture the Scottish literary tradition fostered by Hamilton, Ramsay, Fergusson and Burns in the eighteenth century and further developed in the twentieth century.

FAMILIAR EPISTLES
BETWEEN
W-- H---- and A-- R---.

EPISTLE I.
W----- H------- to A----- R------.

Gilbertfield June 26th, 1719.

Fam'd and celebrated *ALLAN!*
Renowned *RAMSAY*, canty Callan,
There's nowther Highland Man nor Lawlan,
   In POETRIE,
But may as soon ding down *Tamtallan*
   As match wi' Thee.

FOR ten Times ten, and that's a hunder,
I ha'e been made to gaze and wonder,
When frae *Parnaſsus* thou didst thunder
   With Wit and Skill,
Wherefore I'll soberly knock under,
   And quat my Quill.

      OF

Familiar Epistles
between
W—H--- and *A—R---*

EPISTLE I.
W---- H------- to *A-----R------*
Gilbertfield June 26th, 1719.

O fam'd and celebrated Allan!
Renowned Ramsay, canty callan,
There's nowther Highlandman nor Lawlan,
   In poetrie,
But may as soon ding down Tamtallan
    As match wi' thee.

For ten times ten, and that's a hunder,
I ha'e been made to gaze and wonder,
When frae Parnassus thou didst thunder,
    Wi' wit and skill,
Wherefore I'll soberly knock under
    And quat my quill.

Of poetry the hail quintessence
Thou hast sucked up, left nae excrescence
To petty poets, or sic messens,
    Tho round thy stool,
They may pick crumbs, and lear some lessons
    At Ramsay's school.

Tho Ben and Dryden of renown
Were yet alive in London Town,
Like kings contending for a crown;
    'Twad be a pingle,
Whilk o' you three wad gar words sound
    And best to gingle.

Transform'd may I be to a rat,
Wer't in my pow'r but I'd create
Thee upo' sight the Laureat
    Of this our age,
Since thou may'st fairly claim to that
    As thy just wage.

Let modern poets bear the blame
Gin they respect not Ramsay's name,
Wha soon can gar them greet for shame,
    To their great loss;
And send them a' right sneaking hame
    Be Weeping-Cross.

Wha bourds wi' thee had need be warry,
And lear wi' skill thy thrust to parry,
When thou consults thy dictionary
    Of ancient words,
Which come from thy poetick quarry,
    As sharp as swords.

Now tho I should baith reel and rottle,
And be as light as Aristotle,
At Ed'nburgh we sall ha'e a bottle
    Of reaming claret,
Gin that my haff-pay siller shottle
    Can safely spare it.

At crambo then we'll rack our brain,
Drown ilk dull care and aiking pain,
Whilk aften does our spirits drain
    Of true content;
Wow, Wow! But we's be wonder fain,
    When thus acquaint.

Wi' wine we'll gargarize our craig,
Then enter in a lasting league,
Free of ill aspect or intrigue,
    And gin you please it,
Like princes when met at the Hague,
    We'll solemnize it.

Accept of this and look upon it
With favour, though poor I have done it;
Sae I conclude and end my sonnet,
    Who am most fully,
While I do wear a hat or bonnet,
    Yours — wanton Willy.

Postscript

By this my postscript I incline
To let you ken my hail design
Of sic a lang imperfect line,
    Lyes in this sentence,
To cultivate my dull ingine
    By your acquaintance.

Your answer therefore I expect,
And to your friend you may direct
At Gilbertfield do not neglect
    When ye have leisure,
Which I'll embrace with great respect
    And perfect pleasure.

ANSWER I.
A---- R------ to W------H----------
Edinburgh July 10th, 1719.

Sonse fa me, witty, wanton Willy,
Gin blyth I was na as a filly;
Not a fow pint, nor short hought gilly,
    Or wine that's better,
Cou'd please sae meikle, my dear billy,
    As thy kind letter.

Before a lord and eik a knight
In Gossy Don's be candle light,
There first I saw't and ca'd it right,
    And the maist feck
Wha's seen't sinsyne, they ca'd as tight
    As that on *Heck*.

Ha, heh! thought I, I canna say,
But I may cock my nose the day,
When Hamilton the bauld and gay
          Lends me a heezy,
In verse that slides sae smooth away,
          Well tell'd and easy.

Sae roos'd by ane of well kend mettle,
Nae sma did my ambition pettle;
My canker'd criticks it will nettle,
          And e'en sae be't:
This month I'm sure I winna fettle,
          Sae proud I'm wi't.

When I begoud first to cun verse,
And could your *Ardry Whins* rehearse,
Where *Bonny Heck* ran fast and fierce,
          It warm'd my breast;
Then emulation did me pierce,
          Whilk since ne'er ceast.

May I be licket wi' a bittle,
Gin of your numbers I think little;
Ye're never rugget, shan, nor kittle,
          But blyth and gabby,
And hit the spirit to a tittle,
          Of Standart *Habbie*.

Ye'll quat your quill! That were ill-willy,
Ye's sing some mair yet, nill ye will ye;
O'er meikle haining wad but spill ye,
          And gar ye sour,
Then up and war them a' yet, Willy,
          'Tis in your power.

To knit up dollers in a clout,
And then to eard them round about,
Syne to tell up, they downa lout
          To lift the gear;
The malison lights on that rout,
          Is plain and clear.

The chiels of London, Cam, and Ox,
Ha'e raised up great poetick stocks
Of Rapes, of Buckets, Sarks and Locks,
    While we neglect
To shaw their betters; this provokes
    Me to reflect

On the lear'd days of Gawn Dunkell.
Our country then a tale cou'd tell,
Europe had nane mair snack and snell
    At verse or prose;
Our kings were poets too themsel,
    Bauld and jocose.

To Ed'nburgh, Sir, when e'er ye come,
I'll wait upon ye, there's my thumb,
Were't frae the gill-bells to the drum,
    And take a bout,
And faith, I hope we'll no sit dumb,
    Nor yet cast out.

EPISTLE II.
W---- H------- to A-----R------
Gilbertfield July 24th, 1719.

Dear Ramsay,

When I receiv'd thy kind epistle,
It made me dance, and sing, and whistle;
O sic a fyke, and sic a fistle
    I had about it!
That e'er was Knight of the Scots Thistle
    Sae fain, I doubted.

The bonny lines therein thou sent me,
How to the nines they did content me;
Tho', Sir, sae high to compliment me,
    Ye might defer'd,
For had ye but haff well a kent me,
    Some less wad ser'd.

With joyfou heart beyond expression,
They're safely now in my possession:
O gin I were a winter-session
          Near by thy lodging,
I'd closs attend thy new profession,
          Without e'er budging.

In even down earnest, there's but few
To vie with Ramsay dare avow,
In verse, for to gi'e thee thy due,
          And without fleetching,
Thou's better at that trade, I trow,
          Than some's at preaching.

For my part, till I'm better leart,
To troke with thee I'd best forbear't;
For an' the fouk of Ed'nburgh hear't,
          They'll ca' me daft,
I'm unco' irie and dirt-feart
          I make wrong waft.

Thy verses, nice as ever nicket,
Made me as canty as a cricket;
I ergh to reply, lest I stick it,
          Syne like a coof
I look, or ane whose poutch is picket
          As bare's my loof.

Heh winsom! How thy saft sweet stile,
And bonny auld words gar me smile;
Thou's travel'd sure mony a mile
          Wi' charge and cost,
To learn them thus keep rank and file,
          And ken their post.

For I maun tell thee, honest Allie,
I use the freedom so to call thee,
I think them a' sae bra and walie,
          And in sic order
I wad nae care to be thy vallie,
          Or thy recorder.

Has thou with Rosycrucians wandert?
Or thro' some doncie desart danert?
That with thy magick, town and landart,
               For ought I see,
Maun a' come truckle to thy standart
               Of poetrie.

Do not mistake me, dearest heart,
As if I charg'd thee with black art;
'Tis thy good genius still alart,
               That does inspire
Thee with ilk thing that's quick and smart,
               To thy desire.

E'en mony a bonny knacky tale,
Bra to set o'er a pint of ale:
For fifty guineas I'll find bail,
               Against a bodle,
That I wad quat ilk day a mail,
               For sic a nodle.

And on condition I were as babby,
As either thee, or honest *Habby*,
That I lined a' thy claes wi' tabby,
               Or velvet plush,
And then thou'd be sae far frae shabby,
               Thou'd look right sprush.

What tho young empty airy sparks
May have their critical remarks
On thir my blyth diverting warks;
               'This sma presumption
To say they're but unlearned clarks,
               And want the gumption.

Let coxcomb criticks get a tether
To ty up a' their lang loose lether;
If they and I chance to forgether,
               The tane may rue it,
For an' they winna had their blether,
               They's get a flewet.

To learn them for to peep and pry
In secret drolls 'twixt thee and I;
Pray dip thy pen in wrath, and cry,
    And ca' them skellums,
I'm sure thou needs set little by
    To bide their bellums.

Postscript

Wi' writing I'm so bleirt and doited,
That when I raise, in troth I stoited;
I thought I should turn capernoited,
    For wi' a gird,
Upon my bum I fairly cloited
    On the cald eard.

Which did oblige a little dumple
Upon my doup, close by my rumple:
But had ye seen how I did trumple,
    Ye'd split your side,
Wi' mony a long and weary wimple,
    Like Trough of Clyde.

ANSWER II.
A---- R------ to W------H----------
Edinburgh August 4th, 1719.

Dear Hamilton, ye'll turn my dyver,
My muse sae bonny ye descrive her,
Ye blaw her sae, I'm fear'd ye rive her,
    For wi' a whid,
Gin ony higher up ye drive her,
    She'll rin red-wood.

Said I,—Whisht, quoth the vougy jade,
"William's a wise judicious lad,
Has havins mair than e'er ye had,
    Ill-bred bog-staker;
But me ye ne'er sae crouse had craw'd,
    Ye poor scull-thacker.

It sets you well indeed to gadge!
E'er I t' Appollo did ye cadge,
And got ye on his honour's badge,
    Ungratefou beast,
A Glasgow capon and a fadge
    Ye thought a feast.

Swith to Castalius' fountain-brink,
Dad down a-grouf, and take a drink,
Syne whisk out paper, pen and ink,
    And do my bidding;
Be thankfou, else I'se gar ye stink
    Yet on a midding."

My mistress dear, your servant humble,"
Said I, I shou'd be laith to drumble
Your passions, or e'er gar ye grumble,
    Its ne'er be me
Shall scandalize, or say ye bummil
    Ye'r poetrie.

Frae what I've tell'd, my friend may learn
How sadly I ha'e been forfairn,
I'd better been a yont side Kairn-
    amount, I trow;
I've kiss'd the taz like a good bairn."
    Now, Sir, to you.

Heal be your heart, gay couthy carle,
Lang may ye help to toom a barrel;
Be thy crown ay unclowr'd in quarrel,
    When thou inclines
To knoit thrawn gabbed sumphs that snarl
    At our frank lines.

Ilk good chiel says, Ye're well worth gowd,
And blythness on ye's well bestow'd,
'Mang witty Scots ye'r name's be row'd,
    Ne'er fame to tine;
The crooked clinkers shall be cow'd,
    But ye shall shine.

Set out the burnt side of your shin,
For pride in poets is nae sin,
Glory's the prize for which they rin,
           And fame's their jo;
And wha blaws best the horn shall win:
           And wharefore no?

Quisquis vocabit nos vain-glorious,
Shaw scanter skill, than *malos mores*,
Multi et magni men before us
           Did stamp and swagger,
Probatum est, exemplum Horace,
           Was a bauld bragger.

Then let the doofarts fash'd wi' spleen,
Cast up the wrang side of their een,
Pegh, fry and girn wi' spite and teen,
           And fa a flyting,
Laugh, for the lively lads will screen
           Us frae back-biting.

If that the gypsies dinna spung us,
And foreign whiskers ha'e na dung us;
Gin I can snifter thro' mundungus,
           Wi' boots and belt on,
I hope to see you at St. Mungo's
           Atween and Beltan.

EPISTLE III.
W---- H------- to A-----R------
Gilbertfield August 24th, 1719.

Accept my third and last essay
Of rural rhyme, I humbly pray,
Bright Ramsay, and altho it may
           Seem doilt and donsie,
Yet thrice of all things, I heard say,
           Was ay thought sonsie.

Wherefore I scarce cou'd sleep or slumber,
Till I made up that happy number,
The pleasure counterpois'd the cumber,
        In every part,
And snoov't away like three hand omber,
        Sixpence a cart.

Of thy last poem, bearing date
August the Fourth, I grant receipt;
It was fae bra gart me look blate,
        'Maist tyne my senses,
And look just like poor Country Kate
        In Lucky Spence's.

I shaw'd it to our Parish Priest,
Wha was as blyth as gi'm a feast;
He says, Thou may had up thy Creest,
        And craw fu' crouse,
The poets a' to thee's but jest,
        Not worth a souce.

Thy blyth and cheerfu' merry Muse,
Of complements is sae profuse,
For my good Haivens dis me roose
        Sae very finely,
It were ill breeding to refuse
        To thank her kindly.

What tho sometimes in angry mood,
When she puts on her barlick-hood,
Her dialect seem rough and rude,
        Let's ne'er be flee't,
But take our bit, when it is good,
        And buffet wi't.

For gin we ettle anes to taunt her,
And dinna cawmly thole her banter,
She'll take the flings, verse may grow scanter,
        Syne wi' great shame
We'll rue the day that we do want her,
        Then wha's to blame?

But let us still her kindness culzie,
And wi' her never breed a toulzie,
For we'll bring aff but little spulzie,
    In sic a barter,
And she'll be fair to gar us fulzie,
    And cry for quarter.

Sae little worth's my rhyming ware,
My pack I scarce dare apen mair,
Till I take better wi' the lair,
    My pen's sae blunted;
And a' for fear I file the fair,
    And be affronted.

The dull draff drink makes me sae dowff,
A' I can do's but bark and yowff,
Yet set me in a Claret Howff,
    Wi' fowk that's chancy,
My Muse may len me then a gowff
    To clear my fancy.

Then Bacchus like I'd bawl and bluster,
And a' the Muses 'bout me muster,
Sae merrily I'd squeeze the cluster,
    And drink the grape;
'Twad gi' my verse a brighter lustre,
    And better shape.

The pow'rs aboon be still auspicious
To thy atchievments maist delicious,
Thy poems sweet, and nae way vicious,
    But blyth and canny,
To see I'm anxious and ambitious
    Thy Miscellany.

A' blessings Ramsay on the row,
Lang may thou live, and thrive, and dow,
Until thou claw an auld man's pow;
    And thro' thy Creed
Be keeped frae the wirricow,
    After thou's dead. Amen.

ANSWER III.
A---- R------ to W------H----------
Edinburgh September 2d, 1719.

My trusty Trojan,
Thy last oration orthodox,
Thy innocent auldfarren jokes,
And sonsie Saw of Three provokes
    Me anes again,
Tod Lawrie like to loose my pocks,
    And pump my brain.

By a' your letters I ha'e red,
I eithly scan the man well bred,
And sodger wha for honour led
    Has ventur'd bauld;
Wha now to youngsters leaves the yed
    To 'tend his fald.

That bang'ster Billy Caesar July,
Wha at Pharsalia wan the tooly,
Had better sped, had he mair hooly
    Scamper'd thro' Life,
And 'midst his glories sheath'd his gooly,
    And kiss'd his wife.

Had he like you, as well he cou'd,
Upon Burn Banks the Muses woo'd,
Retir'd betimes frae 'mang the crowd,
    Wha'd been aboon him?
The Senate's durks, and faction loud,
    Had ne'er undone him.

Yet sometimes leave the riggs and bog,
Your howms, and braes, and shady scrog,
And helm-a-lee the claret cog,
    To clear your wit;
Be blyth, and let the warld e'en shog,
    As it thinks fit.

Ne'er fash about your niest year's state,
Nor with superior powers debate,
Nor cantrapes cast to ken your fate,
                There's ills anew
To cram our days, which soon grow late,
                Let's live just now.

When northern blasts the oceans snurl,
And gars the heights and hows look gurl,
Then left about the bumper whirl,
                And toom the horn,
Grip fast the hours which hasty hurl,
                The morn's the morn.

Thus to Leuconoe sang sweet Flaccus,
Wha nane e'er thought a gillygacus,
And why should we let whimsies bawk us,
                When joy's in season,
And thole sae aft the spleen to whauk us,
                Out of our reason?

Tho I were Laird of tenscore acres,
Noding to jouks of hallenshakers,
Yet crushe'd wi' humdrums, which the weaker's
                Contentment ruines,
I'd rather roost wi' causey-rakers,
                And sup cauld sowens.

I think, my friend, an fouk can get
A doll of rost beef pypin het,
And wi' red wine their wyson wet,
                And cleathing clean,
And be nae sick, or drown'd in debt,
                They're no to mean.

I red this verse to my ain kimmer,
Wha kens I like a leg of gimmer,
Or sic and sic good belly timmer;
                Quoth she, and leugh,
"Sicker of thae winter and simmer,
                "Ye're well enough.

My hearty goss, there is nae help,
But hand to nive we twa maun skelp
Up Rhine and Thames, and o'er the Alp-
              pines and Pyrenians,
The chearfou carles do sae yelp
                To ha'e 's their minions.

Thy raffan rural rhyme sae rare,
Sic wordy, wanton, hand-wail'd ware,
Sae gash, and gay, gars fouk gae gare,
                To ha'e them by them,
Tho gaffin they wi' sides sae sair,
                Cry—"Wae gae by him!

Fair fa that sodger did invent
To ease the poets toil wi' print;
Now, William, wi' maun to the bent,
                And pouss our fortune,
And crack wi' lads wha're well content
                Wi' this our sporting.

Gin ony sour-mou'd girning bucky
Ca' me conceity keckling chucky,
That we like nags whase necks are yucky,
                Ha'e us'd our teeth:
I'll answer fine,—"Gae kiss ye'r lucky
                "She dwells i' Leith."

I ne'er wi' lang tales fash my head,
But when I speak, I speak indeed:
Wha ca's me droll, but ony feed,
                I'll own I am sae,
And while my champers can chew bread,
                Yours—ALLAN RAMSAY

A
NEW EDITION
OF THE
LIFE
AND
HEROICK ACTIONS
OF THE RENOUN'D
Sir *William Wallace*,
GENERAL and GOVERNOUR
OF
𝔖𝔠𝔬𝔱𝔩𝔞𝔫𝔡.

Wherein the Old obsolete Words are rendered more Intelligible; and adapted to the understanding of such who have not leisure to study the Meaning, and Import of such Phrases without the help of a Glossary.

GLASGOW,

Printed by WILLIAM DUNCAN, *A.D.*
M. DCC. XXII.

EXTRACT FROM HAMILTON OF GILBERTFIELD'S VERSION OF BLIN HARY'S
The Life and Heroick Actions of the Renouned
Sir William Wallace

FROM BOOK VI, CHAPTER II
THE BATTLE OF BIGGAR

There rose the battle, there the warriors tend,
A thousand deaths on thousand wings ascend;
Swords, shields, and spears in mix'd confusion glow.
The field is swept, and lessens at each blow.
Wallace's helm distinguish'd from afar,
Tempests the field, and floats amid'st the war;
Imperious death attends upon his sword,
And certain conquest waits her destin'd lord.
Fierce in another quarter Kent employs
The wrathful spear, nor fewer foes destroys;
Where'er he conquering turns, recedes the foe,
And thickened troops fly open to his blows;
His bounding courser thundering o'er the plain
Bears his fierce rapid lord o'er hills of slain;
Scarce can the weak retreating Scots withstand
The mighty sweep of the invader's hand.
Wallace beheld his fainting squadron yield,
And various slaughter spread along the field,
Furious he hastes, and heaves his orbed shield,
Resolv'd in arms to meet his enemy.
Before his spear they rush, they run, they fly.
And now in equal battle meet the foes.
Long lasts the combat, and resound their blows:
Their dreadful faulchions brandishing on high.
In wavy circles heighten to the sky;
With furious ire they run the field around,
And keen on death, explore each secret wound.
They heave, they pant, they beat in every vein,
While death sits idle on the crimson plain.
Long in suspense the uncertain battle hung,
And fortune, fickle goddess, doubted long

On whom she should the laurel wreath bestow,
Whom raise as conqueror, whom depress as foe.
At last the Hero, tir'd with forc'd delay,
At his full stretch rose, and with mighty sway,
Bore from the foe his shield's defence away.
Now high in air the shiny sword he rear'd,
Ponderous with fate the shiny sword appear'd:
Descending full, it stops his stifled breath;
Giddy, he turns around, and reels in death.
The stringy nerves are wrapt around in gore,
And rushing blood distain'd his armour o'er.
Now all is death and wounds; the crimson plain
Floats round in blood, and groans beneath its slain.
Promiscuous crowds one common ruin share,
And death alone employs the wasteful war.
They trembling fly by conquering Scots oppress'd,
And the broad ranks of battle lie defac'd;
A false usurper sinks in ev'ry foe,
And liberty returns with every blow.
Before their prince the mangled subjects die,
The slaughter swells, and groans ascend the sky.
The king beheld with sad astonished eyes,
The havock of the various battle rise:
Unable to sustain, fain would he stay,
And yet again retrieve the vanquish'd day.
At last, behind his back he threw the shield,
Spurs on his rapid steed, forsakes the field.
The Scots pursue, and follow fast behind;
The rattling noise swells dreadful in the wind.
With grief, Longcastle saw the foul retreat,
Restrain'd their flight, and durst prolong their fate.
"Whence does our hearts this coward terror know,
Defeat ne'er stain'd our conqu'ring arms till now:
Stay recreant, stay, nor thus ignoble fly,
But bravely conquer, or yet bravely die."
Scarce had he spoke, when quiv'ring all with fear,
'Scap'd from the foe, two fugie friends appear:
"Stop, stop!" they cried, "your hasty flight restrain,
And with swift vengeance meet your foes again;
Opprest with wine the Scottish heroes lie,
And feel the soft effects of luxury.
With ease we may return again, and spread
The crimson plain around with heaps of dead." ⌘

BIBLIOGRAPHICAL NOTES

The texts of the *Familiar Epistles between William Hamilton and Allan Ramsay* printed here are from the separate pamphlet edition, Edinburgh, [?] 1719, with variants and modernising of capitalisation, italicisation, some of which are taken from the Scottish Text edition of *The Works of Allan Ramsay*, Volume I, edited by John Burns Martin and John Walter Oliver, 1945, who used the quarto subscribers' edition of Ramsay's *Poems*, 1721, which was "Printed by Mr Thomas Ruddiman, for the Author" and has re-set texts of the *Epistles*.

I have chosen the later edition of 1719 rather than the marginally earlier edition as my copy-text, because it has the additional stanza for Ramsay's "Answer I" that begins "Before a lord and eik a knight". I have reproduced some pages from the edition that I have used as copy-text, taking them from the full texts of the *Epistles* reproduced in my *Four Poets of Cambuslang*, 1996. Ramsay's *Poems* of 1720 reprints, or gathers in, several pamphlets including that of the *Epistles*. It was only with the quarto subscribers' edition, 2 volumes 1721, 1728, that Ramsay put together a "formal" edition of his poems. The full Scottish Text Society edition comprises six volumes with volumes I (n.d.) and II, 1953, edited by Martin and Oliver and volumes III to VI edited by Alexander Manson Kinghorn and Alexander Law, 1961, 1970, 1972, 1974.

The subscribers' list of the 1721 quarto edition gives 476 names and others are known to have subscribed. Lieutenant William Hamilton is a subscriber and others who may have Cambuslang connections are: Mr Archibald Hamilton, who could be the Rev Hamilton who had owned Gilbertfield and Westburn; Alexander Hamilton of Dechmont, although there is more than one Dechmont; and Colonel Montgomery who could be of Newton, Cambuslang. Sir William Maxwell of Calderwood is certainly a near neighbour of the poet of Gilbertfield and, amongst the long list of members of the peerage, there is His Grace the Duke of Hamilton. Somewhat unexpectedly, the poet of Gilbertfield is not listed as a subscriber to volume two, 1728, of Ramsay's *Poems* but Mr Alexander Pope and Sir Richard Steele did subscribe to both volumes.

Like that of his pamphlet editions, the publication history of *The Tea-Table Miscellany*—reprinted twelve times during Ramsay's lifetime and twenty-four times in the eighteenth century—is very complicated. In his authoritative bibliography John Burns Martin gave 1724 as the date of the first edition but a unique copy dated 1723 is now in Yale; the National Library of Scotland has a photocopy of this edition.

For "A Bibliography of the Writings of Allan Ramsay" by John Burns Martin, first published in 1931, see the revised version in Ramsay's *Works*, vol. VI, Scottish Text Society, 1974. For biography see: the

Scottish Text Society volumes; Burns Martin, *Allan Ramsay: A Study of His Life and Works*, Cambridge, Massachusetts, 1931; and Allan H. MacLaine, *Allan Ramsay*, Boston, 1985.

William Hamilton's "Epistles to Ramsay", "The Last Dying Words of Bonny Heck, A Famous Grey-Hound in the Shire of Fife" and "Willie was a wanton wag" are printed in *Four Scottish Poets of Cambuslang & Dechmont Hill 1626-1990*, edited with an introduction by Duncan Glen, Edinburgh, Akros, 1996. In addition to Hamilton the other three poets are: Rev Patrick Hamilton (minister at Cambuslang 1626-1645); John Struthers born in East Kilbride and poet of Dechmont Hill (1776-1853); and Duncan Glen (born in Cambuslang in 1933).

The first edition of William Hamilton's version of Hary's *Wallace* was printed in Glasgow by William Duncan, 1722, in a foolscap 8vo edition (165mm). The translator's Dedication to the Duke of Hamilton is dated, Gilbertfield, 21st Sep. 1721. Following many years of neglect, there is now an edition published in 1998, and reprinted in 1999, in Edinburgh by Luath Press, with an Introduction by Elspeth King in which she writes that "from 1722 until the edition of 1859, Hamilton's *Wallace* went through another twenty-three editions, all of them printed in Scotland, except for that issued by WW Crawford of New York in 1820." The most recent scholarly edition of Hary's *Wallace* was edited by Matthew P. McDiarmid, 2 Volumes, Edinburgh, Blackwood for the Scottish Text Society, 1968, 1969. D.G. ⌘

LIST OF SUBSCRIBERS

Mrs Carol Allan
William Anderson
Harold Ayres
A. Azma

David Baillie
S. J. Beecroft
Moira Bowkett
Norman Brown
George Buckmaster
John D. Burton

Robert Russell Calder
Mrs Helen Cameron
Gerard Carruthers
John Corbett

W. Davidson
Peter Davis
Tom Dickie
Michael Dineen
Donald Docherty
Richard T. Doyle
Peter Dunbar
Sarah Dunnigan

Edinburgh City Libraries

William Flitcroft
B. Foster
Mrs Margaret N. Frood

Alison and Ian Glen
Mrs Morag Glen
Alastair Green
James Greene

Mrs Sylvia Hamilton
Stewart Hannan
Gillian Henderson
Peter Henderson
Eleanor J. Howie

D.R. Inglis

Stuart James

Malcolm Keen
Brian Keenan
Bernard Kellett
Alison and Andrew Kelly
Elizabeth King

G. F. Lawrence
Brian Lawson
John Letham
Robert Letham
William Lilly
Maurice Lindsay

Neil R. MacCallum
Doreen McCann
J. Derrick McClure
Duncan MacGregor
Laurie Jane MacGregor
S. MacNeil

Douglas Mack
Lloyd Martin
Hugh T. Metcalfe
William Miller
John Milne
R.K.D. Milne

Archie Montgomery
Charles K.D. Munro

Brigadier J.M. Neilson, C.Eng, MIEE

Melvyn and Christine Partington
Mrs A. Paterson
Mrs Sheena Pawson

Harold Ray
Joan and Trevor Rees
Alison Rider
David Robb
Leonard Roberts
John Robertson

Mrs Catherine J. Scott
Hilary Scott
Scottish Poetry Library
Raymond Sears
Avril Seed

Kenneth Simpson
Alan Smith
David Smythe
Miss Yarrow Spenser
Colin Stephens
David Stephenson
Wm. N. Stevenson
Mrs Jill F. Stockdale
Alan Stone
John Stuart
Clifford Sutherland

J.M. Tate
Darrall Taylor
R. Todd

Gavin Waddell
Rev. Alan H. Ward
Tom Watson
Alex Wilson
Robert Wiseman

Other subscribers wish to remain anonymous.